Original title:
Letting Go

Copyright © 2024 Swan Charm
All rights reserved.

Author: Johan Kirsipuu
ISBN HARDBACK: 978-9916-79-009-0
ISBN PAPERBACK: 978-9916-79-010-6
ISBN EBOOK: 978-9916-79-011-3

Embrace the Open Sky

Beneath the azure, dreams take flight,
Wings spread wide, hearts feel so light.
Clouds drift softly, a warm embrace,
Freedom dances, in endless space.

Sunrise whispers, a brand new start,
Chasing shadows, mending the heart.
In every breeze, hope's gentle sigh,
Here we stand, to embrace the sky.

Dandelions on the Wind

Little seeds floating, poised to roam,
Carried by breezes, far from home.
Whispers of wishes, softly they're spun,
Each tiny puff, a tale begun.

Fields adorned in golden light,
Dandelions dance, a pure delight.
Embracing moments, wild and free,
Together we weave, our destiny.

Casting Shadows to the Past

Memories linger, shadows may sway,
Echoes of laughter, drifting away.
Time's gentle hands, they mold and bend,
In fading light, we find our mend.

Reflections glimmer, on waters still,
Each silent thought, a haunting thrill.
Casting our dreams to the night's vast sea,
The past speaks softly, setting us free.

Farewell to Faded Dreams

Once bright and vibrant, dreams took flight,
Now whispers linger, fading from sight.
Memories blend, like colors in haze,
A bittersweet song, in twilight's gaze.

Yet hope remains, a flickering flame,
In the heart's chamber, it calls out your name.
With each new dawn, we learn to believe,
Farewell to the past, it's time to achieve.

Moments Dispersed

In the hush of twilight's gleam,
Memories float like a dream.
Whispers dance upon the air,
Time draws close, yet lingers there.

Silent echoes of the past,
Fleeting shadows, never cast.
Sunrise breaks, a canvas wide,
Painting life, with hope as guide.

Fragments woven, hearts entwined,
Every laughter we have signed.
Minutes shift like grains of sand,
Moments cherished, hand in hand.

A Breeze of New Beginnings

Gentle winds caress the morn,
With each breath, the day is born.
New horizons come in sight,
Chasing dreams into the light.

Leaves unfurl, the world awakes,
Every promise, hope remakes.
Tides of change are flowing free,
In the heart, we find the key.

Birds in flight, they soar and sing,
Celebrating everything.
Letting go of what's behind,
Embracing all that's yet to find.

Farewell to Yesterday

As the sun begins to set,
I whisper low, I won't forget.
You've shaped the path I tread,
In my heart, your echoes spread.

Shadows long, the night draws near,
In my soul, I hold you dear.
Every tear and every smile,
Carried with me for a while.

Close the book, but do not weep,
For the dreams we dared to keep.
Farewell, dear friend, I must move on,
In my heart, you'll never be gone.

Empty Nest Serenade

In the stillness of the eve,
Whispers of the past reprieve.
Nests once filled with laughter clear,
Now hold echoes, soft and near.

Feathers scattered, dreams take flight,
In the twilight, hearts ignite.
Though the silence may seem vast,
Love remains, a bond unsurpassed.

Windows open, breezes sigh,
Chasing clouds across the sky.
In the quiet, we will find,
Hope resides within the mind.

A Journey Beyond Familiar Shores

Beyond the waves where quiet calls,
Adventures dance on breezy thralls.
With every tide, new tales unfold,
As dreams set sail, our hearts be bold.

The sun dips low, a golden hue,
It whispers softly, skies so blue.
Each moment sweet, with laughter shared,
Our spirits soar, the past we bared.

Through stormy seas and starry nights,
We navigate by hopeful lights.
Each port we greet, new friends we find,
The world expands, our hearts entwined.

The taste of salt, the wind's embrace,
In every journey, we find grace.
With every wave, we rise and fall,
Together we answer adventure's call.

So fear not change, for life is grand,
A journey waits, just take my hand.
Beyond the shores, our spirits free,
Together we make history.

Withering Chains

In shadows deep, where silence sighs,
A heart confined, it yearns to rise.
The chains of doubt, they clink and cling,
Yet hope, like spring, begins to sing.

With every tear, a remedy found,
The weight of fears begins to drown.
A whisper breaks, the light draws near,
And in that glow, I shed my fear.

The bonds that bind begin to fray,
With every step, I find my way.
The path of courage leads me on,
Through darkest nights, I greet the dawn.

No longer trapped in shadow's hold,
My spirit sings, my heart is bold.
The chains are dust, I break away,
With every breath, I seize the day.

So let the world, with its demands,
Feel the strength of open hands.
With withering chains cast to the ground,
In newfound freedom, life is found.

A Canvas of Moving On

In strokes of color, life unwinds,
A canvas vast, where hope aligns.
With every fade, a new hue spreads,
As past regrets slip from our heads.

The brush of time paints fresh designs,
Each moment bold, and love entwines.
The scars of loss become the art,
A masterpiece that's born from heart.

With gentle hands, we dare to dream,
Creating visions, bright and gleam.
In every shade, a lesson learned,
In every curve, our spirits turned.

As seasons change, and colors blend,
A story told without an end.
With every layer, freedom calls,
To dance in light as darkness falls.

So pick your colors, paint your way,
With every choice, a brighter day.
A canvas waits, so let it show,
The beauty found in moving on.

Fragile Threads Unraveled

In twilight's embrace, we find our way,
Tangled dreams weave, starting to fray.
Hope flickers gently, like a lone flame,
Each moment whispers, calling our names.

Fingers brush softly, past shadows of doubt,
In silence, we wander, lost in the rout.
Yet through the fabric, a tapestry glows,
Resilience unfurls, as the spirit flows.

A fragile connection, each heartbeat we share,
The threads of our lives, beyond time and air.
Though storms may come crashing, we stand side by side,

Together, unbroken, with arms open wide.

The Art of Surrender

In the gentle dusk, we learn to let go,
Trusting the tides, where the wild winds blow.
With every release, a new path is drawn,
Beneath the soft cloak of a quiet dawn.

The weight of the world fades into the past,
Each moment a canvas, no shadows are cast.
In stillness, we listen, the heart's quiet song,
Resilience grows deep, where we all belong.

Letting time dance, like leaves in the breeze,
Embracing the rhythm, we find our ease.
The art of surrender, a beautiful grace,
In the vastness of now, we discover our place.

Embracing the Empty

In the hollow spaces, calm waters flow,
Embracing the empty, a chance to grow.
Where silence resides, we learn to ignite,
A spark of creation, born from the night.

Life's fleeting currents, a canvas so bare,
In absence, we find what we choose to share.
With open hearts, we start to unfold,
A story untold, a treasure of gold.

In shadows of solitude, courage takes flight,
Each moment a promise, a beacon of light.
Embracing the empty, we fill it with dreams,
Crafting our futures, or so it seems.

Echoes of Freedom

In the boundless sky, where dreams take their flight,
Echoes of freedom dance in the night.
With whispers of hope, each star finds its way,
Painting the cosmos, where shadows can't stay.

The wind carries tales of those once confined,
Breaking the silence, unchained, unlined.
In every heartbeat, a rhythm we share,
In echoes of freedom, we rise from despair.

A chorus of voices, entwined in the air,
Vibrating softly, a song we all bear.
With wings made of courage, we soar from the ground,
In harmony's cradle, our spirits are found.

Tides of Transformation

Waves crash on the shore,
Each grain a story told.
Change sweeps like the tide,
New beginnings unfold.

Voices whisper in the breeze,
Revealing dreams yet born.
The moon pulls at our hearts,
Guiding us with its charm.

Time dances in the sand,
Footprints slowly fade.
Yet in our hearts we know,
The journey's never made.

Seas of doubt may rise high,
But hope is ever near.
For with each ebb and flow,
We calm our deepest fears.

Embrace the change within,
Let go of what's behind.
The tides are calling you,
To seek what you may find.

Pieces of the Past

Faded photographs lie still,
Captured smiles and tears.
Fragments of a life once lived,
Echoes through the years.

Moments stitched in memory,
Like threads of fragile lace.
Sewn into the fabric,
Of time and sacred space.

Lessons learned from love once lost,
Bitter and yet sweet.
Each scar tells a story,
Of how we rise to meet.

In shadows of remembrance,
We find the light to guide.
For every piece that breaks,
Creates a new inside.

So treasure all the fragments,
Of who you used to be.
For in the pieces of the past,
You find your harmony.

Transitions of the Heart

Feelings shift like the seasons,
Gentle winds of change.
New loves spark a fire,
In hearts once feeling strange.

Whispers of a new beginning,
Call from deep within.
Embrace the sweet unknown,
Let the journey begin.

Trust the rhythm of the pulse,
As it swells and flows.
For every beat we journey,
A deeper love it sows.

In the quiet of our souls,
We dance beneath the stars.
Each step a tiny promise,
No distance is too far.

So let the heart keep moving,
Unlock the hidden door.
Transitions weave our stories,
In love forevermore.

The Sound of Silence

In the stillness of the night,
Whispers softly sigh.
Echoes from the shadows,
A world that feels nearby.

Silence wraps around my soul,
A blanket made of dreams.
In this quiet sanctuary,
Nothing's as it seems.

Thoughts rise like the morning mist,
Fleeting as a breeze.
In the sound of silence,
I find my heart at ease.

Voices fade into the dark,
In stillness, I can hear.
The melody of hope unfolds,
A song that feels so clear.

So treasure each tender pause,
For therein lies the truth.
In the sound of silence,
We reconnect with youth.

Lanterns Set Afloat

In the night, lanterns glow,
Carried by whispers, soft and slow.
Each light a wish, set free to roam,
Guiding lost souls gently home.

Rippled waters catch the gleam,
Reflecting dreams, a tranquil theme.
Stars above in silent cheer,
Dance with hope brought ever near.

Voices echo, softly call,
In this moment, we are all.
Bound by light, a shared embrace,
Floating on in this sacred space.

Lanterns flicker, secrets share,
In the stillness, hearts laid bare.
Each craft a story, a cherished part,
Of life's journey, a work of art.

Threads of Fate Untwined

In the loom of life, threads weave tight,
Colors mingling, dark and bright.
Each twist and turn, a path explored,
Woven stories, hearts restored.

Eager hands with gentle care,
Pull the yarn with love to spare.
Fate's design, both cruel and kind,
Interlaced, our lives aligned.

Moments shared, connections made,
In the tapestry, no need to fade.
Every sorrow and every joy,
Becomes a thread, each heart a ploy.

As the patterns start to show,
Lessons learned, we come to know.
With every stitch, we find our place,
In this fabric of time and space.

The Turning of the Leaves

Golden hues, the leaves descend,
Whispers of change, a quiet end.
In crisp air, they dance and sway,
Marking the close of summer's play.

Twilight settles on the ground,
Rustling softly, nature's sound.
Branches bare, yet spirits rise,
In every color, the heart complies.

Gathered round, we share our tales,
Of summers past and autumn gales.
Each leaf that falls holds a refrain,
Of moments cherished, joys and pain.

Seasons turn, a cycle's grace,
In every change, we find our place.
With each rustle, a promise shines,
Renewal waits in the changing lines.

Whispers of Release

In the silence, secrets lie,
Softly sighing, letting go high.
Gentle breezes carry dreams,
Unraveled hopes, like flowing streams.

Tethered hearts find strength to bend,
In the shadows, light can mend.
What was held can now be free,
In the stillness, we can see.

Every fear, a fleeting thought,
In the tapestry, we are caught.
With every breath, we shed our chains,
Embrace the burdens, release the reins.

Nights grow long, the dawn will break,
From the depths, our spirits wake.
With whispers soft, we set our sights,
On brighter paths, new daylights.

The Stillness of Release

In the cool embrace of night,
Whispers dance, taking flight.
Chains that bound now softly break,
In the stillness, hearts awake.

Moonlight bathes the weary soul,
Filling cracks, making whole.
Gentle sighs escape the lips,
Freedom found in tender grips.

Waves of doubt begin to clear,
As hope rises, drawing near.
Tides of past no longer bind,
In release, a peace we find.

Softly now, the world unwinds,
Joy in each moment reminds.
Letting go of all that weighs,
In stillness, lost in sunray's haze.

Breathe deeply, let worries cease,
In this dance, discover peace.
Through the quiet, spirits soar,
In stillness, we are evermore.

Storms Passing

Dark clouds gather, shadows loom,
Thunder rumbles, nature's boom.
Yet within the fierce embrace,
Calm will come to take its place.

Raindrops drum a rhythmic tune,
Whispers of a coming moon.
Lightning flashes, bright and bold,
Tales of nature's fury told.

Time will turn the tide of fear,
Beneath chaos, truth is clear.
Every storm will meet its end,
Storms may rage, but skies can mend.

In the aftermath, we find,
Lessons left, both strong and kind.
With each drop, the earth will sing,
Renewal in the life we bring.

So we stand through winds that howl,
Remembering the roaring growl.
Embrace the calm on the sea,
Peace awaits, just let storms be.

Finding Quiet in the Chaos

Amidst the noise, a still small voice,
Inviting us to make a choice.
To step away from frantic pace,
And find our true, authentic space.

Fractured moments swirling round,
In the chaos, peace is found.
Pause a while, let tensions melt,
In the silence, strength is felt.

Mindful breaths as shadows cast,
Letting go of burdens past.
In the whirlwind, soft reprieve,
A gentle heart begins to weave.

Nature's call, a whispering breeze,
In the quiet, senses tease.
Find the calm beneath the storm,
In stillness, we begin to warm.

So linger in the spaces wide,
Where chaos fades and dreams abide.
In the quiet, we reclaim,
A sacred spark, a tender flame.

Resilience in the Turning

Winds may howl, and trees may sway,
Life will dance, in its own way.
Through the trials, we grow strong,
Resilience sings the ancient song.

Roots dig deep in troubled ground,
With each challenge, life abounds.
Seasons shift, and storms will pass,
In the turning, we find our path.

Embers glow in fading light,
Fueling hope through the darkest night.
Every leaf that falls shall rise,
With each dawn, new dreams arise.

Strength resides in every heart,
In the struggle, we find our part.
With each turn, we learn to stand,
Together as we hand in hand.

So let the seasons come and go,
In the dance of high and low.
Resilience blooms, a vibrant fall,
In the turning, we answer the call.

Fleeting Moments

In the blink of an eye, they pass,
Tiny echoes lost in the grass.
Laughter mingles with the breeze,
Time ticks softly, never to seize.

A glance exchanged, a fleeting touch,
Memory held, but never too much.
Footsteps fading, whispers near,
Moments cherished, forever dear.

Painted skies at the close of day,
Colors swirl and softly sway.
The sun dips low, a warm embrace,
Each second carved, a sacred space.

Stars awaken, the night unfolds,
Tales of wonder yet untold.
In shadows cast, dreams take flight,
Fleeting moments shape the night.

Countless stories in this dance,
Catch the spark, give life a chance.
With every heartbeat, treasures gleam,
In fleeting moments, we find our dream.

Fragments Adrift

Scattered pieces in the tide,
Waves of memory collide.
Lost and found, they twist and twirl,
Fragments of a drifting world.

Echoes whisper on the shore,
Tales of sorrow, hopes, and lore.
In the silence, secrets weave,
Fragments adrift, learn to believe.

Colors bleed, the canvas torn,
Stories written, hearts reborn.
Every shard holds a glint of light,
A puzzle waiting for the right sight.

Take a breath, let the waves roll,
Find the pieces that make you whole.
In the chaos, beauty stays,
Fragments adrift in life's maze.

Hands reach out, yearning to find,
Connections made, souls intertwined.
Together we create and sift,
In fragments adrift, we all lift.

The Whisper of Change

Leaves tremble in the gentle breeze,
Nature's language speaks with ease.
A rustle here, a shiver there,
The whisper of change fills the air.

Morning light breaks the night's embrace,
Flickering shadows in every space.
With each dawn, the world reclaims,
Through soft echoes, life re-names.

Time flows like a river's course,
Turning tides with unseen force.
Embracing change, we all must grow,
In whispered tones, new paths will show.

Moments shift, like sands of time,
In the silence, life's rhythm chimes.
A call to rise, to dare, to dream,
In the whisper of change, we gleam.

Let go of fears, let hope ignite,
In the twilight, hearts feel light.
For every ending, something new,
The whisper of change calls to you.

Unseen Horizons

Beyond the mountains, far and wide,
Lies a journey where dreams abide.
With every step, the heart will roam,
To unseen horizons, we find our home.

The sun sets low, a radiant hue,
Painting skies in vibrant blue.
In the distance, shadows play,
Unseen horizons beckon the day.

Whispers of dreams fill the air,
Promises linger, a call to dare.
With courage bold, we sail the tides,
To unseen horizons, where hope resides.

Stars align in the night's embrace,
Guiding hearts to a sacred place.
With each horizon, mysteries grow,
Unseen paths, where passions flow.

In the silence, the heartstrings pull,
Every sunset makes the soul full.
With open arms, we chase our flight,
To unseen horizons, our guiding light.

Sails on the Horizon

Canvas billows in the breeze,
Waves embrace the quiet seas.
A distant call from skies of blue,
Adventure whispers, 'Come, pursue.'

Sunrise paints with golden hue,
Fleeting dreams, a journey new.
Bound by wind, we roam so free,
Sails unfold our destiny.

Guided by the stars above,
Hearts ablaze with hope and love.
Every moment, a chance to steer,
Through the vastness, without fear.

Time flows gently, waves reflect,
In the silence, we connect.
Drifting onward, a tranquil dance,
Sails unfurled, we take the chance.

Beneath the sky, the horizon gleams,
Together we follow our dreams.
With every knot, our spirits rise,
Sailing on, toward the skies.

Heartstrings Unbound

In the echoes of soft sighs,
Whispers dance beneath the skies.
Fingers brush like velvet threads,
In this place where love spreads.

Moments weave a tapestry,
Moments shared, you and me.
With each heartbeat, fondness grows,
In this bond, the world glows.

Eyes meet in a timeless gaze,
Lost together in love's maze.
In every laugh, in every tear,
Our heartstrings pull, drawing near.

Through the storms and sunny days,
We find strength in lovely ways.
Together facing night and dawn,
In the flow, our worries gone.

Though the road may twist and bend,
We are journeying, my friend.
In the spaces we both fill,
Heartstrings unbound, love stands still.

The Weightless Flight

Letting go of all that weighs,
Drifting free in sunlit rays.
With each breath, I rise and glide,
In this peace, I choose to hide.

Clouds embrace the azure sky,
On this journey, we can fly.
Wings of dreams begin to soar,
Leaving doubt upon the shore.

Gravity fades, I feel alive,
In the air, my spirit thrives.
With the wind, I weave the light,
Into realms of endless flight.

Every heartbeat sings a tune,
In the warmth of afternoon.
Floating gently, hearts unite,
Dance with joy in weightless flight.

In this moment, we are free,
Finding joy, just you and me.
Through the clouds, together high,
In the vastness, we can fly.

Seasons of Transition

Leaves transform in vibrant hues,
Whispers carried in the blues.
Nature shifts with gentle grace,
In each change, we find our place.

Winter's chill gives way to spring,
Hope renewed, the heart takes wing.
Blossoms bloom in warm embrace,
In the light, we find our pace.

Summer sun brings laughter's tune,
Days stretch long under the moon.
In the warmth, our spirits rise,
Dancing boldly, touching skies.

Autumn's breath, a soft goodbye,
Golden fields beneath the sky.
Harvest dreams, we gather near,
In the cycle, love sincere.

Time flows on like rivers run,
Seasons change, the heart's undone.
Through each phase, we learn to grow,
In transition, love will flow.

The Weight of Wings

In skies where dreams ascend,
The burdens softly cling,
A dance of hope and fear,
Embracing the weight of wings.

Through tempests fierce and wild,
The heart learns how to soar,
Yet anchored by the past,
A struggle to explore.

With every feather lost,
A story left behind,
In silence they still speak,
Of journeys intertwined.

When twilight whispers low,
And shadows stretch their hands,
We carry all our dreams,
Like footprints in the sands.

The sky a canvas vast,
With colors yet unseen,
In the weight of wings we find,
The strength to chase the dream.

Fading into the Light

As dusk embraces day,
The shadows start to blend,
A gentle sigh of warmth,
Where endings meet the bends.

In whispers soft and low,
The stars begin to gleam,
Each flicker tells a tale,
Of hope within a dream.

The heart remembers well,
The glow of yesteryears,
Yet bravely moving forth,
While shedding silent tears.

Caught in twilight's grace,
We dance on edges bright,
With every step we take,
We are fading into light.

So let the darkness breathe,
And guide us with its song,
For even in the night,
We learn where we belong.

Unbound Horizons

The endless stretches call,
To wander far and wide,
In every breath we take,
The world becomes our guide.

With open hearts we sail,
Across the azure sea,
Each wave a whispered dream,
That sets our spirits free.

The mountains stand so tall,
As guardians of the land,
They teach us how to climb,
And reach for what we planned.

In valleys rich and green,
We find our grounded place,
With every step we take,
We cherish time and space.

From sunrise into dusk,
Unbound horizons gleam,
In the journey of our souls,
We forge the truest dream.

Heartstrings Loosened

With threads of love entwined,
Our hearts have found their song,
Yet seasons change like tides,
And we must carry on.

The laughter once we shared,
Now echoes in the breeze,
As memories float past,
Like leaves upon the trees.

In tender moments brief,
We learned to let things go,
Yet in the strands of time,
Our stories softly flow.

For every tear we shed,
A lesson lingers near,
In heartstrings loosened loose,
We find the path so clear.

So here we stand unbound,
And cherish all we knew,
With love that lasts beyond,
The skies of every hue.

Dance of the Unanchored

In twilight's embrace, shadows sway,
Whispers of winds, guiding their play.
Where tides pull free, and dreams take flight,
Souls untethered, lost in the night.

With open hearts, they spin and twirl,
Stars above mirror their graceful whirl.
Each movement a story, untold and wild,
In freedom's dance, the earth is beguiled.

A rhythm born from restless seas,
An echo of laughter carried by breeze.
No anchors weigh them, no chains confine,
In the dance of the unanchored, they shine.

They glide through starlight, chasing the dawn,
In every flicker, a new path drawn.
With every leap, the world feels new,
In this cosmic waltz, they break through.

Upon the horizon, where sky meets sand,
Their spirits soar, hand in hand.
With every heartbeat, they weave their art,
Embracing the chaos, they live from the heart.

The Driftwood's Journey

Once a sturdy branch, now adrift,
Carried by currents, a watery gift.
Through storms it wanders, through calm it roams,
Finding new shores, as it seeks a home.

The sea tells tales of places unknown,
Each wave a story, a journey grown.
Whispers of sand, kisses from air,
The driftwood dances without any care.

In tides of change, it learns to bend,
Though battered and weary, it will not end.
For every ebb, there's a swell to rise,
In rootless freedom, it claims the skies.

Sunlight glistens on weathered bark,
The soul of the sea leaves its mark.
With each gentle push, it finds its way,
In nature's cradle, it longs to stay.

And when at last, it greets the shore,
The driftwood rests, its journey bore.
In branches wide, life will begin,
In harmony found, it will dance again.

Collecting Shattered Pieces

In fragments of dreams, we search the ground,
For pieces of hope, so scarcely found.
With tender hands, we gather the shards,
A mosaic of heartache, crafted with guards.

Each splinter reflects, a story untold,
Of battles lost, and courage bold.
We weave with care, the broken and whole,
Reclaiming the fragments that once formed a soul.

Like glass in the light, they shimmer and gleam,
Transforming the sorrow into a dream.
A tapestry woven with threads of the past,
In collecting the pieces, we find peace at last.

From ashes we rise, with strength renewed,
In every fracture, a chance to be viewed.
With love in the cracks, we embrace the scars,
In the shards of our lives, we find who we are.

So let us not fear the paths we create,
With shattered pieces, we dance at fate.
For in the chaos, beauty will shine,
In collecting the pieces, our hearts will align.

Unfastening the Heart

In silence wrapped, the heart stays bound,
Tethered by fears that weigh it down.
With each gentle breath, a whisper starts,
To unravel the ties that hold the heart.

Softly it yearns for the light of day,
To shake off the shadows, to find its way.
Through the seams of doubt, it seeks to break,
The chains of the past, for freedom's sake.

So one by one, the knots come undone,
As courage swells with the rising sun.
Each heartbeat a promise, a step to depart,
In the journey of unfastening the heart.

No longer confined, it begins to soar,
Exploring horizons, longing for more.
In the depths of its truth, it finds its grace,
In the unfastening, it finds its place.

A chorus of hope now fills the air,
With love as the compass, it knows no despair.
In unfastening, it learns to ignite,
The flame of its spirit, embracing the light.

Threads of Time Frayed

Moments weave like fragile threads,
Caught in the whispers of our dreams.
Time, a swift and ruthless river,
Pulls us along its endless streams.

Fragments of joy and sorrow blend,
Echoes of laughter, shadows of tears.
Each stitch a story, each knot a bend,
Woven together through all these years.

Days drift like leaves on autumn's breeze,
Falling softly, drifting apart.
Yet memories linger, like a tease,
An ever-present, tender heart.

In the tapestry of life we find,
Patterns formed from love and strife.
Though threads may fray, they're intertwined,
A legacy of our shared life.

So hold on tight, as time unfolds,
Embrace the moments, let them soar.
For in each thread, a tale is told,
Of dreams once lost, and dreams in store.

Flickering Flames to the Stars

Fires burn low with a gentle glow,
Whispers of warmth in the night air.
Dancing shadows, soft and slow,
Memories flicker without a care.

Stars above with glimm'ring grace,
Watch the embers twinkle and sway.
In the dark, we find our place,
As dreams and flames together play.

Each flame a wish, a story bright,
Carried on winds of the silent wait.
Soon to be born in the soft moonlight,
Fueling the hopes we cultivate.

Together we stand, hand in hand,
Guided by the light that we seek.
In the glow, our hearts expand,
Finding the strength in each heartbeat.

So let the flames reach up high,
To the heavens where wishes roam.
For in the sparks, dreams never die,
They find the stars and call them home.

Bridges Burnt and Reclaimed

Fires raged, the bridges fell,
A past in ruins, shadows cast.
In silence echoes the farewell,
As ashes settle, memories last.

Yet hope takes flight on trembling wings,
From remnants rise the seeds of change.
What once was lost, the heart still sings,
In the reclamation, we rearrange.

Each step forward, a chance to heal,
Through broken paths, we redefine.
What once felt cold begins to feel,
Like warmth that seeps into our spine.

With every bridge that we restore,
Connections forged in light anew.
From burnt remains, we build once more,
A future bright, a bond that's true.

So look ahead with courage clear,
Embrace the scars that shape the way.
For in each bridge, we hold what's dear,
The past informs the path we lay.

Serenade of Solitude

In quiet corners, shadows meet,
The whispers of the night unfold.
A serenade of soft retreat,
Where secrets linger, shy and bold.

The moon, a guide through silent hours,
Lends her light to hearts that yearn.
In solitude, we find our powers,
A space to heal, a place to learn.

With every note, the silence breaks,
A symphony of thoughts laid bare.
In solitude, the spirit wakes,
Finding strength in the still air.

Though longing brushes by the soul,
Embrace the quiet, let it sing.
In the hush, we feel more whole,
A gentle balm through suffering.

So here I dwell, with heart wide open,
In moments sweet, I choose to stay.
For in solitude, my fears are broken,
And I find peace in every sway.

Radiance in the Unknown

In shadows deep, where secrets lie,
A flicker glows, a gentle sigh.
We chase the whispers of the night,
In search of hope, in search of light.

The stars above, they pull us near,
Each twinkle holds a hidden cheer.
Beyond the veil, where dreams can roam,
Unfold the paths that lead us home.

With every step, we fear and crave,
The mystery that we can't save.
Yet still we tread through doubts we face,
In the unknown, we find our grace.

Embrace the void, let courage swell,
For in the dark, new stories tell.
The radiance born from hearts that dare,
Illuminates the paths we share.

Fluid Threads of Existence

In tides that turn, we drift and flow,
A woven dance, a natural show.
Each moment threads a vibrant hue,
In life's embrace, it welcomes you.

The rivers run, with tales to weave,
Through valleys wide, in hearts they cleave.
A gentle pull, a mighty surge,
Connected souls, in love emerge.

With every breath, we intertwine,
The sacred bonds of yours and mine.
In fluid grace, our spirits soar,
Through endless currents, evermore.

The dance of fate, a lively jest,
In the tapestry, we find our quest.
Through joy and pain, we find our way,
In fluid threads, we learn to stay.

The Dance of Departure

A final bow, the curtains close,
In silent grace, the journey goes.
With heavy hearts, we let things be,
Embracing all, both you and me.

The echoes linger in the air,
In every glance, a poignant stare.
Yet in this parting, seeds are sown,
In every end, new paths are grown.

With every tear that bids goodbye,
A chance to rise, to learn to fly.
The dance may pause, but spirits rise,
In whispered dreams beneath the skies.

Let memories weave a tender thread,
To guide us forth, where paths are led.
For in each step, we carry light,
The dance of love, through day and night.

Sails Set Free

With winds of change, the sails unfurl,
As ships embark on ocean's swirl.
Each journey calls, with dreams in sight,
To chart the course, to chase the light.

The horizon waits, a canvas wide,
In tranquil seas, our hopes abide.
Each wave a chance, to rise and roam,
With sails set free, we find our home.

The storms may rage, the skies may cry,
Yet through the tempest, we learn to fly.
With courage bold, we navigate,
In the heart's compass, we find our fate.

As stars align, our spirits soar,
Through every port, we seek and explore.
In every journey, love's decree,
Forever bound, our sails set free.

Unclenched Fists

In shadows cast by silent war,
We stand with hearts that long for more.
Let go of doubt, let courage rise,
Unclench the hands, embrace the skies.

The battles fought, the scars we wear,
Each mark a tale, a journey's dare.
To lift our voices, strong and free,
In unity, we find our glee.

With every breath, we shed our chains,
A symphony of hope remains.
Together we shall break the mold,
With unclenched fists, our dreams unfold.

In peaceful stances, here we stand,
Transform the anger, heal the land.
Through open palms, let kindness flow,
The world can change, if we bestow.

As dawn ignites the darkened night,
We'll rise as one, a radiant light.
With hearts aglow, we'll face the mist,
In this embrace, no clenched fists.

Wildflowers in Abandon

Among the rocks, where rivers curl,
A field of dreams, wildflowers whirl.
Each petal bright, a story speaks,
In vibrant hues, the valley peaks.

With careless grace, they dance and sway,
Unfazed by storms, they find their way.
In splendor bold, a sight unplanned,
Their fleeting beauty, forever grand.

The sunlit paths, where shadows play,
No chains to bind, they drift away.
In whispers soft, the breezes call,
Wild and free, they break the fall.

With roots unchained, they seek the light,
In every hue, a pure delight.
These blooms of hope, in every glance,
Remind us all, to take a chance.

In nature's hands, we find our peace,
Their silent language grants release.
A hopeful heart, a soul set free,
Wildflowers in abandon, we see.

The Art of Unburdening

In whispered thoughts, we find the space,
To let it go, to find our grace.
Release the weight, the heavy chain,
In silence, soothe the nagging pain.

With gentle hands, we craft our sighs,
The tears we shed, the truths, the lies.
Each moment shared, a brushstroke bright,
In canvas clear, reveal the light.

The burdens lifted, life feels new,
With open hearts, we step to view.
The colors blend, the shadows fade,
In artful ways, we won't evade.

Through stories told, and laughter shared,
We find the joy, the love declared.
The art of unburdening unfolds,
With every breath, our life beholds.

So shed the past, embrace the now,
In every step, we'll take a bow.
For in this dance, the soul will sing,
The art of life, what joy it brings!

Moments Left Behind

A fleeting glance, a touch, a smile,
The moments pass, they linger awhile.
In memories etched, we find our ground,
The echoes softly, like whispers sound.

From laughter shared, to tears we shed,
The paths we walked, the words unsaid.
In time's embrace, we hold them dear,
Moments left behind, yet ever near.

In twilight's glow, the shadows blend,
Each heartbeat counts, the ties, the mend.
We carry forth the tales we weave,
In every breath, we choose to believe.

The seasons shift, but still we find,
The fragments of our lives entwined.
In quiet grace, we'll honor time,
These moments left behind, sublime.

As we advance, with steps so bold,
We cherish stories that we've told.
The past, the present, a tapestry,
In moments left behind, we're free.

Unfolding into Dusk

The sun dips low beneath the trees,
Whispers linger in the gentle breeze.
Shadows stretch and colors blend,
As day concedes, and night begins.

Stars awaken, one by one,
The canvas dark, a life undone.
In quiet moments, dreams take flight,
Embracing all, the coming night.

The horizon glows, a fiery kiss,
A fleeting moment, filled with bliss.
In twilight's embrace, we find our way,
To chase the light, then fade to gray.

Crickets sing their evening song,
In nature's hush, we all belong.
Heartbeats echo through the air,
As dusk reveals the world laid bare.

Beneath the stars, our hopes will dance,
In the stillness, we take a chance.
The dusk unfolds its tender grace,
A new beginning, time and space.

Echoes of Voices Lost

In hallways steeped in whispered dreams,
Voices linger, or so it seems.
They weave through air with a soft touch,
Fading shadows, we miss so much.

Letters penned on fragile scrolls,
Fragments left to fill the holes.
In echoes past, we seek the truth,
Reminders of our distant youth.

Ghostly laughter haunts the night,
Carried forth by the moon's light.
Time may take, but can't erase,
The memories that time can't face.

In the stillness, we hear their call,
A gentle reminder, we had it all.
Through veils of silence, love remains,
In echoes of joy, in echoes of pains.

Collecting whispers from the past,
Holding tightly to moments that last.
In the heart, these voices play,
Guiding us along the way.

Serpentining Paths Ahead

Winding trails beneath the trees,
Each twist and turn brings gentle ease.
Footsteps lead to dreams unknown,
With every step, new seeds are sown.

In shadows deep, the path may veer,
Yet with each choice, we shed our fear.
Curves and bends unveil the view,
Landscapes shift, a vibrant hue.

Past the mountains, through the vale,
Carrying stories in every trail.
The future beckons, bold and bright,
As we journey toward the light.

Nature whispers, guiding hands,
Through hidden dreams and shifting sands.
With every curve, a chance to grow,
A tapestry of life to sow.

Trust the compass deep within,
Feel the pulse, let the adventure begin.
For serpentining paths will always show,
The way to places we long to go.

The Space Between Chapters

Between the pages, silence reigns,
In the pauses, life explains.
Moments gathered, thoughts arise,
In the margins, reach for skies.

Words unspoken, hints of fate,
Echoes of a dream wait.
In the breath before the next,
Lies the truth of what connects.

Turning leaves, the ink still fresh,
New tales waiting to enmesh.
In the gaps, our hearts will soar,
Seeking more than was before.

The interludes, a cherished space,
Where hope and longing find their place.
With each chapter, a piece of time,
A rhythm set, a soul's pure rhyme.

So linger here, in tender pause,
In the quiet, we find our cause.
Embrace the shift, the coming change,
For life unfolds, rich and strange.

Emptiness as a Friend

In quiet hours, I sit alone,
The whispers of void, a gentle tone.
Emptiness wraps like a warm embrace,
In shadows, I find my hidden space.

A silent partner, it holds me tight,
In the absence of sound, I find my light.
It calms the chaos, stills the mind,
In the depths of nothing, comfort I find.

With each heartbeat, the void expands,
An echo of dreams in empty lands.
I learn the language of silent sighs,
And weave my thoughts into the skies.

A friend in darkness, it knows my name,
In the dance of dusk, I feel no shame.
From emptiness flows an endless stream,
A canvas untouched, the start of a dream.

So I embrace this silent ride,
With emptiness walking by my side.
In its gentle grip, I find my way,
A soothing balm for the fray of day.

Drifting Leaves

In autumn's breath, the leaves descend,
With each soft swirl, they twist and bend.
Gold and crimson, they dance with grace,
Fading whispers of summer's embrace.

They tumble down on gentle breeze,
A fleeting sight that aims to please.
Like memories lost in the passage of time,
Each leaf tells a story, a silent rhyme.

The trees stand bare, in solitude,
While leaves share tales of gratitude.
They laugh and spin, in a final show,
Before they rest in the earth below.

Nature's art, in colors bold,
Each leaf a treasure, a story told.
As they drift away, set free from care,
They whisper secrets to the chilled air.

In their descent, a lesson clear,
Letting go brings a joyous cheer.
For in their falling, they find their peace,
And from their end, new lives increase.

Cloak of Solitude

A cloak of solitude drapes around,
In silence, my solace can be found.
The world retreats into hidden shade,
Where thoughts wander and dreams are laid.

In the gentle hush, I find my voice,
A quiet heart, a mindful choice.
Moments linger, like stars in the night,
Wrapped in stillness, I feel the light.

With every breath, the loneliness sings,
Of hidden joys that silence brings.
I embrace the stillness, the calm so deep,
In the warmth of solace, I softly seep.

Outside, the chaos roars and raves,
But here in solitude, my spirit saves.
A tender shield against the storm,
In this quiet haven, I feel so warm.

Within this cloak, I find my peace,
The weight of the world begins to cease.
In solitude's arms, I learn to be free,
An open heart, just me and me.

The Shift of Seasons

As winter fades and spring draws near,
The world awakens, shedding fear.
Buds unfurl, in vibrant hues,
A dance of life, the earth renews.

Summer's warmth soon takes its place,
With golden rays that softly trace.
Fields of green sway in the sun,
Nature whispers, the cycle's begun.

Then autumn brings a cooling sigh,
Leaves turn crimson, bidding goodbye.
A tapestry of change unfolds,
In every hue, a story told.

The shift of seasons, a timeless flow,
A reminder of life's ebb and glow.
In each transition, magic resides,
As time dances, and the heart abides.

With every season, lessons learned,
In nature's rhythm, my spirit turned.
To cherish moments, fleeting, bright,
In the shift of seasons, find my light.

The Freedom of Departures

In distant lands where dreams take flight,
We leave behind the day's last light.
With whispered hopes and tender sighs,
We chase the stars across the skies.

Each step we take, a story spun,
The journey calls; we can't outrun.
With every heartbeat, shadows fade,
As new horizons beckon, made.

The past may tug, a gentle chain,
Yet forward is where we must remain.
With winds of change in every breath,
We find our peace amidst the rest.

Unfolding paths, uncharted ways,
In golden sun or silver haze.
With courage found in each goodbye,
We rise to meet the endless sky.

In moments lost, we find our strength,
To soar beyond all boundless length.
The freedom found in letting go,
Is like the tides that ebb and flow.

Ashes of Memory

Within the ember's glow so bright,
Lie whispers of a faded night.
Each spark a tale of love once shared,
Now scattered winds, in silence bared.

Through smoky veils of what has been,
Echoes dance where dreams have seen.
Fragments linger in the air,
Of laughter lost, of tender care.

In sepia tones, the mind will weave,
The moments cherished, hard to leave.
Yet time, relentless in its quest,
Turns memory to gentle rest.

With every sigh, a shadow plays,
A fading song from ancient days.
The ashes linger, softly warm,
Reminding us where love once swarmed.

Yet in the cinders' quiet grace,
We find the strength to face our place.
Though memory fades, its heart remains,
In whispers of the soul's refrains.

Rivers Running Away

Beneath the trees where shadows grin,
The rivers flow, with tales within.
They carve the earth with gentle hands,
And sing a song of distant lands.

Each twist and turn, a secret keeps,
In murmurs low where nature sleeps.
They chase the sun, they flee the night,
And shimmer bright with silver light.

Through valleys deep and mountains high,
They wander forth, they dream, they sigh.
With every bend, a journey made,
Through sun-kissed fields and twilight's shade.

But oh, the tales they leave behind,
In currents strong, in echoes blind.
For rivers run but never stay,
Forever bound to flow away.

Yet still they dance, unfurling grace,
Embracing change in their own pace.
And though they may not linger long,
Their songs inspire where hearts belong.

The Last Embrace

In twilight's glow, we find our place,
Two souls entwined in the last embrace.
With whispered words and tearful eyes,
We hold the night as time complies.

Each heartbeat echoes stories shared,
In tender silence, love declared.
With every sigh, the world stands still,
As dreams converge on this sacred hill.

Through fleeting moments, soft and rare,
We find a solace in the air.
With hands held tight, we face the dawn,
As shadows fade, and life moves on.

Yet in this pause, a timeless grace,
Our hearts forever feel the trace.
Of promises made in quiet tones,
A bond that dances, never alone.

So let the night unfold its wings,
As love remains in whispered things.
For in this last embrace, we find,
A love eternal, intertwined.

Whispers of Release

In twilight's gentle hue, we remain,
Silent confessions float like autumn leaves.
Hearts unburdened, free of their chain,
Embracing the breezes, the soul retrieves.

Whispers of dreams ride the cool night air,
Listen closely; they carry our song.
A melody woven with tender care,
Echoing softly where we both belong.

The stars gather close, twinkle and gleam,
Casting shadows of hopes long held dear.
In the darkness, we'll dare to dream,
Far from the noise, we've nothing to fear.

Each moment a treasure, each breath a chance,
To step into freedom, let our hearts soar.
With every heartbeat, a graceful dance,
In whispers of release, we seek for more.

The Weight of Unraveled Threads

A tapestry spun from moments passed,
Fragile fibers, they fray at the seams.
Each thread whispers stories, echoes cast,
As we weave the fabric of forgotten dreams.

Under the weight of choices made,
Silently, burdens cling to weary backs.
In the quiet, hope and fear parade,
Through each crowded thought, the mind relax.

The sun sets softly on untold fears,
Tracing paths where memories once lay.
In the stillness, we wipe away tears,
Unraveling threads in the fading day.

With every pull, a liberation gained,
Letting go of what no longer thrives.
In the spaces where silence has reigned,
We find the strength that truly survives.

Echoes of Yesterday

In the corners of time, shadows dance still,
Whispers of laughter, a soft, fleeting glow.
Here lies the warmth of a heart's gentle thrill,
Carried on winds where the sweet memories flow.

Each echo resounds, a bittersweet song,
Tales of the past wrapped in shimmering light.
Together we journey, though days may be long,
Through echoes of yesterday, we take flight.

Let the moments entwine, soft as a vow,
Through laughter and sorrow, we cherish the blend.
In each fragile sigh, we remember just how,
Time, like an artist, shapes hearts to mend.

An hourglass spilling with dreams intertwined,
Marked by remembrance, our footprints remain.
In each fleeting heartbeat, the past is enshrined,
Echoes of yesterday, love won't wane.

The Softness of Farewell

In the silent hour when shadows grow long,
We gather our thoughts like leaves in the breeze.
A bittersweet melody plays our song,
As we say farewell beneath the tall trees.

Nostalgia lingers, a gentle embrace,
In the warmth of the sunset's fading ray.
Every goodbye holds a trace of grace,
Leaving us richer for the words we say.

Through whispered goodbyes, hearts intertwine,
Cherished connections woven in time.
Though paths may diverge, love's thread will align,
In the softness of farewell, we still climb.

With eyes turned to horizons yet unseen,
We carry the laughter that filled our days.
In the tapestry of life, we glean,
The softness of farewell in countless ways.

Fragments in Flight

Across the sky, they drift away,
Carried lightly on wings of day.
Whispers of dreams in the softest glow,
Scattered pieces of long-lost flow.

Through the azure, they weave and dance,
In every twirl lies a fleeting chance.
Moments captured, then set free,
In the vastness, just you and me.

Echoes of laughter, a soft refrain,
Floating like feathers in gentle rain.
With every gust, new tales are spun,
Fragments of life, together as one.

Under the stars, they shimmer bright,
Each a beacon in the deep of night.
A constellation of all we've known,
In this canvas, we've brightly grown.

In every flutter, a memory stays,
Marking the path of our wandering ways.
Fragments of time, in the silent hush,
Painting our stories, in a golden rush.

Hearts in the Breeze

In the whisper of trees, hearts begin to sway,
Carried on breezes that guide their play.
Each gentle gust stirs emotions wide,
Binding us close, like the turning tide.

With every flutter of a leaf above,
Nature breathes softly, echoing love.
A silky caress of the evening air,
Kindred spirits in a dance of care.

Moments of silence beneath the stars,
Hearts resonate like forgotten guitars.
Melodies rise in the twilight's embrace,
Revealing the wonder in each crafted space.

Through the stillness, sweet promises flow,
Hearts entwined as the soft winds blow.
In the dawn's light, we'll take to flight,
Chasing the dreams that ignite the night.

Together we journey, two souls in the breeze,
Finding solace in nature's sweet tease.
Hearts in the wind, we soar and glide,
In a world turned vibrant, forever side by side.

Lightening the Load

With each step forward, burdens untie,
Shed like leaves beneath a clear sky.
The weight of worries begins to shift,
As moments of joy become our gift.

In the laughter shared, our spirits rise,
Casting away shadows, we touch the skies.
Together we lighten what once felt grand,
Finding solace in a helping hand.

The journey ahead may still feel steep,
But lightness follows where memories leap.
With every smile, a burden released,
In the warmth of friendship, we find our peace.

Through trials faced, we carry the flame,
Lighting the path in a world untamed.
Hope blossoms bright when shared on our way,
In the bonds we forge, we can always stay.

So let us remember, as days unfold,
Together we carry, together we hold.
With each step lighter, our hearts align,
In the dance of life, our spirits shine.

The Final Goodbye

In the quiet of dusk, we gather near,
Words unspoken weigh heavy with fear.
With tear-stained faces, we breathe in the air,
Knowing this moment, so fragile, so rare.

The echoes of laughter shatter the night,
Memories flicker, like stars burning bright.
Each shared glance carries warmth of the past,
A bond never broken, forever to last.

But in this farewell, we find our release,
Embracing the whispers that offer us peace.
The journey continues beyond what we know,
As love transcends time, and spirits will glow.

With every heartbeat, we hold you so tight,
Though distance may part us, love's pure light.
Guides us through shadows, a glow in the night,
In the realm of the heart, you remain in our sight.

As we say goodbye, a promise we make,
To cherish your memory, never forsake.
In every sunrise, in each gentle sigh,
You're forever with us, our ultimate tie.

Breathing in New Beginnings

With dawn's light, a whisper calls,
New paths await, as darkness falls.
Each breath taken, a seed that's sown,
In the heart's garden, hope is grown.

The sky paints dreams in hues so wide,
We shake off shadows, let fears slide.
Embrace the change, let spirits soar,
In every moment, there's so much more.

The fresh scent of morning dew,
Tells tales of all that we can do.
With open hearts, we venture free,
In this landscape of possibility.

Let laughter echo, let joy resound,
In every corner, magic's found.
Breathing in, this brand new chance,
Together we step, in life's dance.

A canvas blank, a story untold,
In every heartbeat, courage bold.
With each new dawn, let life expand,
Breathing in new beginnings, hand in hand.

The Gentle Unraveling

In twilight's hush, the world slows down,
Whispers of soft, a tranquil sound.
Threads of worry slowly cease,
In the calm, we find our peace.

The tapestry of thoughts unwind,
With every sigh, we leave behind.
A gentle touch, a quiet grace,
In this moment, we find our place.

Like petals falling from a flower,
Releasing time, embracing power.
The storm inside begins to fade,
In stillness, the heart is laid.

Through woven dreams, we start to tread,
Unraveling fears, moving ahead.
In letting go, we rise anew,
A softer world, in shades of blue.

With gentle hands, we mold our fate,
Embracing love, learning to wait.
As night dissolves and dawn draws near,
In the gentle unraveling, we find cheer.

Surrendering the Shoreline

Waves crash gently against the land,
Footprints fade as time slips sand.
With each retreat, the tide reveals,
Secrets buried, the heart conceals.

In surrender, we find a space,
To dance with dreams, to embrace grace.
The ocean's song, a soft refrain,
Calls to the soul, like gentle rain.

As horizons stretch, horizons blend,
In the ebbing tides, we learn to mend.
What once was lost can still be found,
In the dance of waves, we are unbound.

The sea of change, an endless roam,
In every drop, we find our home.
Letting go, we float with ease,
Surrendering the shoreline, we find peace.

Trusting currents, we rise and fall,
In this rhythm, we hear the call.
With open hearts, we journey wide,
Surrendering the shoreline, side by side.

When Chains Turn to Feathers

In shadows deep, the coldness binds,
Heavy hearts with tangled minds.
Yet in that darkness, a spark ignites,
When chains turn to feathers, we take flight.

A whisper soft, a glimmer bright,
Promising freedom, the end of night.
With every breath, we shed our weight,
In this release, we redefine fate.

The stories told of struggles past,
Now woven wings, our spirits cast.
What held us down now lifts us high,
When chains turn to feathers, we touch the sky.

With courage born from pain's embrace,
We find our voice, we find our place.
In laughter's light, our burdens cease,
When chains turn to feathers, we find peace.

So spread your wings, let spirits soar,
For in each heart, there's so much more.
With strength renewed, we rise above,
When chains turn to feathers, we choose love.

Gentle Farewell

The sun dips low, a final sight,
Whispers linger, softly bright.
Memories dance in fading light,
Goodbye is near, yet hearts take flight.

With every sigh the moments fade,
Warmth of bond, a serenade.
Though paths may part, we're not afraid,
In echoes sweet, love's serenade.

Time gently steals, yet love remains,
In silent tears, we break our chains.
A tender glance, the heart retains,
In whispered words, affection reigns.

So hold me close, this fleeting chance,
In our farewell, let spirits dance.
With every beat, our souls entranced,
A gentle pause, love's last romance.

Ashes of Attachment

Memories lie like scattered dust,
In shadows cast, we fade to rust.
Brittle fragments, dreams adjust,
In the cold void, we learn to trust.

From embers glows the past's embrace,
Yet all we have is empty space.
The warmth we knew, a lost trace,
In lingering thoughts, we chase the grace.

Letting go, a bittersweet song,
With every note, we feel we're strong.
Yet in the stillness, something's wrong,
As ashes rise, we hum along.

Rivers of change run deep and wide,
Leaving behind what could not bide.
Through tangled roots, we start to glide,
In the ashes, our hearts confide.

Dancing with the Wind

The breeze calls out, a gentle sway,
As leaves take flight, they weave and play.
In soft embrace, we drift away,
With laughter light, we greet the day.

With open arms, we spin and glide,
The world feels bright, with dreams as guide.
In whispered tunes, our hearts collide,
Together lost, like fate applied.

Through fields of green, our spirits chase,
As sunlight casts its warm embrace.
We lose ourselves in nature's grace,
With every step, we find our place.

So let us dance, the world our stage,
In wild abandon, we turn the page.
Boundless laughter, free from cage,
In every move, let joy engage.

Unclasping Hands

Fingers intertwine, a tender hold,
In moments sweet, our story told.
Yet time draws near, its chill so bold,
As hearts resist, the warmth turns cold.

With fragile ease, we start to part,
A silent ache within the heart.
Gentle whispers, where love's an art,
In every beat, we feel the start.

Promises linger like evening light,
Yet shadows stretch, consuming bright.
In every space, the echoes fight,
As hope grows dim, we search for flight.

So here we stand, in quiet grace,
Two souls entwined in time and space.
Unclasping hands, we feel the trace,
Of love that bloomed, now a soft place.

A Canvas Left Blank

A canvas lies bare, untouched by the hand,
Whispers of color, dreams yet unplanned.
Each stroke a choice, a flicker of light,
In silence it waits, for the day to ignite.

Imagined horizons, possibilities vast,
Painted emotions from shadows that cast.
With each brush that glides, a story unfolds,
In the void of the waiting, a masterpiece molds.

The palette is ready, just add to the scene,
Vivid and lively, a whispered routine.
From starkness blooms beauty, chaos can sing,
A canvas now dances, unfurling its wing.

As hues intertwine, the heartbeats align,
Each color a heartbeat, a rhythm divine.
In layers of patience, the magic begins,
A canvas transformed, where creation spins.

With courage, we venture where visions collide,
In each stroke, we find what we oft try to hide.
No longer a blank, but a world of embrace,
A canvas alive, finding solace in space.

The Unraveling

Threads pulled apart, in gentle dismay,
Life's fabric is fraying, come what may.
Moments are woven, then slowly unwind,
In the quiet of night, a truth we must find.

The tapestry tells tales of laughter and pain,
Rich with our joy, yet soaked by the rain.
Each knot a reminder, of times that we shared,
In the dance of the heart, we've learning prepared.

As patterns dissolve, new forms shall emerge,
From the scraps of our past, fresh visions surge.
Embracing the chaos, we breathe in the change,
In the unravelling, life feels less strange.

With each thread we lose, new ones we shall gain,
Healing through space, like blossoms from rain.
We stitch with our dreams, anew paths to create,
In every unraveling, we learn to relate.

So let the yarn tangle, let colors combine,
In the art of becoming, our spirits align.
The unravelling beckons, a journey, not end,
Through the beauty of breach, we find strength to mend.

Memories on the Wind

Soft whispers of moments, carried so far,
Like echoes of laughter, a guiding star.
In the dance of the breeze, old stories revive,
Memories drift gently, reminding us to thrive.

They weave through the trees, in shadows they play,
Echoes of yesterdays, never in gray.
A tapestry woven with joy and with grief,
In the breath of the wind, we seek our relief.

Sunrise and twilight are stitched with our dreams,
Caught in the currents, soft flickering beams.
Time holds our tales, like leaves on the stream,
In the winds of remembrance, a delicate theme.

Every sigh of the breeze carries whispers of old,
In each gust, a treasure more precious than gold.
Fragments of laughter, of love in the air,
Memories like feathers, so light, yet they care.

So listen intently, let the heart be your guide,
To cherish the moments, with arms open wide.
For memories on the wind will find their way back,
Charting our journeys, keeping love on track.

Departures in Dusk

The sky wears a cloak of deep indigo,
As shadows stretch long, the night begins slow.
In parting's embrace, a bittersweet sigh,
Departures in dusk, where goodbyes lie.

The horizon whispers tales of the day,
With stars close at hand, the night leads the way.
Lovers and dreamers, we gather our thoughts,
In the warmth of the twilight, we tie up our knots.

Moments adorned with a golden regret,
The longing for closeness, the time to forget.
Yet each turn of the hour brings hope anew,
In the waning light, we learn how to pursue.

As the sun dips below, the world turns to dream,
In hushed tones, we ponder the life's flowing stream.
Each parting a promise, a seed we plant,
In the twilight's embrace, we breathe in the chant.

So let the dusk cradle what fades from our sight,
Reflecting on memories that sparkle like light.
Departures may linger, yet love holds its place,
In the silence of dusk, we find our own space.

Serenade of the Unheld

In twilight's embrace, whispers arise,
Soft melodies drift beneath the skies.
Hearts beat in rhythm, yet souls stay apart,
Yearning for closeness, a dance of the heart.

The moonlight waltzes on shadows so sweet,
A symphony plays where dreamers meet.
Fingers outstretched, but we never connect,
Love calls in silence, a quiet defect.

Every glance shared, a note in the air,
Unspoken desires linger everywhere.
But time moves swiftly, like clouds in the night,
Craving a warmth that fades from the sight.

In gardens of longing, we wander so free,
Imagining moments that never could be.
Yet hope softly lingers in each faded tune,
A serenade echoing beneath the moon.

So here I stand, with dreams yet unheld,
In the quiet spaces, where passions are meld.
A heart full of music, longing to play,
For the serenade waits at the close of the day.

Echoes of Yesterday

Beneath autumn leaves, shadows dance slow,
Whispers of moments from long ago.
Memories linger in the crisp, cool air,
Each step retracing the paths we once shared.

Time paints in colors that fade and dissolve,
Yet still in the heart, old feelings revolve.
Photographs tucked away in a drawer,
Speak of a time we can't help but adore.

Voices like echoes, they float through the night,
Brought back by dreams that spark in the light.
Each laughter and tear, a note in the past,
In the fabric of life, our moments are cast.

The clock keeps on ticking, relentless and true,
Yet in the stillness, I reach out for you.
Ghosts of our yesterdays softly remind,
That love's sweet refrain is a treasure we find.

So here in the present, I hold on so tight,
To the echoes of yesterday, glowing and bright.
For though we have changed, the heart keeps its tune,
In the depths of our being, under the moon.

The Elusive Horizon

On the edge of dawn, where dreams take flight,
The horizon beckons, a dazzling sight.
Chasing the shadows that dance in the glow,
We yearn for the places we desperately know.

Each step forward whispers of paths yet to tread,
While doubts weave around all the words left unsaid.
But hope is a compass that guides our way,
Through storms and through silence, it shows us the day.

Mountains rise high, like challenges cast,
Each summit we seek is a lesson amassed.
But when we look close, we often foresee,
That the horizon is more than mere fantasy.

With each dawn that breaks, old fears start to fade,
In the space between miles, new dreams are made.
The freedom to wander, to question, to roam,
In the chase of the horizon, we find our true home.

For it's not just the distance that calms the soul,
But the journey itself, the making us whole.
So reach for the skyline, let your spirit soar,
The elusive horizon opens every door.

Beyond the Comfort Zone

In the cocoon of ease, we often reside,
Shying away from the storms outside.
Yet deep in our hearts, a longing prevails,
For the winds of change that carry new tales.

Step forth into shadows, embrace the unknown,
Journeying bravely to places unshown.
With courage as armor, we break every chain,
To dance in the chaos, to learn from the strain.

The walls that protect sometimes stifle our wings,
But beyond with each risk, new freedom springs.
We find strength in struggle, and wisdom in tears,
Transforming our lives, confronting our fears.

So leap into the dark, let the heart be your guide,
In each stride you take, find joy amplified.
For life is a canvas, waiting for bold,
To paint every moment, we must be so bold.

Beyond the comfort, the world is alive,
In the dance of the daring, our spirits will thrive.
So take that first step, let adventure unfold,
For beyond the comfort zone, our dreams can be told.

The Nature of Farewells

Beneath the dusk, we part our ways,
Silent whispers fill the haze.
Memories linger, hearts entwined,
In every shadow, love's designed.

Time steps lightly, yet it pounds,
Each farewell, a loss, resounds.
Laughter echoes in the breeze,
A bittersweet, gentle tease.

The sun sinks low, colors fade,
Old promises softly laid.
With every step, we feel the weight,
Of unspoken dreams that wait.

As night unveils its starry gown,
We wear our smiles like a crown.
In the distance, voices call,
Yet in our hearts, we hold it all.

And so we part, yet not alone,
With tender roots, our love has grown.
In every rise and each goodbye,
We learn to live, to love, to sigh.

Solitary Bloom

In a garden lost to time,
A lone flower dares to climb.
Petals soft, a vibrant hue,
Basking in the morning dew.

The world around may fade away,
Yet still, it dreams of light each day.
With every breeze, it sways with grace,
Rooted firm in its own place.

Seasons change, and storms may brew,
Yet steadfast, it remains true.
In solitude, it finds its song,
A melody the earth prolongs.

From cracks and stones, it breaks the mold,
A tale of bravery, brave and bold.
Each petal whispers secrets deep,
Of promise in the heart, we keep.

Though alone, it stands with pride,
An emblem of the fight inside.
For in the silence, strength will bloom,
In every heart lies its own room.

The Rapture of Release

A tethered heart begins to sigh,
With every breath, it learns to fly.
Chains dissolve in gentle light,
As shadows fade, embraced by night.

Moments trapped in time now free,
Dancing wild, a jubilee.
Whispers of the past recede,
In the stillness, hearts are freed.

The weight once borne becomes a breeze,
As laughter dances through the trees.
Embrace the dawn, let go the night,
In the chaos, find your light.

With every step, unburdened soul,
Wounds will heal, and hope will roll.
The rapture sings in open air,
In every heartbeat, love lays bare.

So let the rivers flow and wind renew,
In essence pure, let life construe.
A symphony of joy unfolds,
In freedom's arms, the heart beholds.

Time's Embrace

In the stillness, seconds fade,
Moments pass, like soft cascade.
Life's sweet rhythm, ebb and flow,
In every heartbeat, love will grow.

Memories dance in twilight hours,
Traces of forgotten flowers.
Laughter lingers in the air,
Time weaves magic everywhere.

Each tick of clock, a whispered truth,
Holding close our fleeting youth.
In twilight's kiss, the world transforms,
As night unveils its cosmic charms.

With every dawn, release the past,
Embrace the present, hold it fast.
Time's embrace, both gentle and fierce,
With every moment, hearts it pierce.

So treasure now, let go the fear,
In time's sweet dance, we find what's dear.
A tapestry woven in grace,
In love's embrace, we find our place.

Roots Untethered

In fields of gold, where shadows play,
I found my dreams in the light of day.
The winds of change began to stir,
Awakening the heart's soft purr.

With every step, I felt the ground,
A strength in roots that knows no bound.
The ties that bind may stretch and strain,
Yet through the storms, I'll rise again.

I cast away the weight of doubt,
Learning what this life's about.
To seek the sun, to dance in rain,
To break the mold and face my pain.

Each flicker of hope, a guiding star,
I journey forth, no matter how far.
The past may linger, but I am free,
To soar beyond what I can see.

Roots untethered, I take flight,
In whirling winds, I find my light.
No chains to hold, no fears to bind,
In every heartbeat, strength I find.

The Silence Between Heartbeats

In whispered dreams, where stillness lies,
A world awakens, hidden from eyes.
The moments caught, a breath held tight,
In silence deep, I find my light.

Each heartbeat measures time's gentle sway,
In spaces vast, we drift away.
A pause, a breath, the world stands still,
In quietude, the heart does fill.

Echoes linger, tales untold,
In secret chambers, the soul unfolds.
The silence speaks in tones so clear,
Whispers of hope that linger near.

Between each beat, a truth revealed,
In quiet moments, the scars are healed.
With every pause, a chance to be,
In silence, I'm set free.

The rhythm flows, and life goes on,
Yet in the silence, I am strong.
A melody of calm I weave,
In the heart's stillness, I believe.

Burdened No Longer

The weight I carried, now laid down,
No more the frown, no need to drown.
Each step I take, a lighter sound,
In freedom's arms, my joy is found.

With echoes past, I learned to fight,
In darkness deep, I sought the light.
The chains of fear, I break away,
Into the dawn of a brighter day.

I shed the layers, one by one,
Reclaim my worth, I am the sun.
The burdens fade like autumn leaves,
In their release, the heart believes.

As shadows shrink and fears dissolve,
I rise anew, I'm free to evolve.
No longer bound by what was known,
In open skies, my spirit's grown.

Burdened no longer, I embrace,
The endless journey, the open space.
With every breath, in strength I find,
A life unchained, a heart unlined.

When the Stars Align

In twilight's glow, our dreams ignite,
A dance of fate in the deepening night.
The universe spins with a whispered sigh,
When stars align, we know we fly.

Paths intertwine, like roots below,
In cosmic rhythms, our spirits flow.
Each heartbeat echoes a secret sign,
In whispers soft, the stars define.

Together we rise, defying the norm,
In bond unbroken, a vibrant form.
Through tempests fierce and tranquil nights,
When stars align, love ignites.

With every glance, a story unfolds,
In celestial maps, our fate behold.
The cosmos sings, a sweet refrain,
When stars align, we break the chain.

In the vast expanse, our dreams take flight,
Boundless together in endless night.
With hearts ablaze, and paths divine,
We chase the magic when stars align.

The Quiet Release

In the hush of nightfall, whispers play,
Soft secrets shared, then drift away.
Beneath the stars, a gentle sigh,
Embracing moments as they fly.

Leaves rustle softly, a tender dance,
Nature's lullaby, a whispered chance.
Holding close what's dear and true,
In the quiet, a heart breaks through.

A fading echo of a distant tune,
Carried by the light of a silver moon.
With every breath, release the pain,
Find solace in the soft refrain.

Together we wander, hand in hand,
In this stillness, we understand.
Each tear, a step toward what can be,
In the quiet, we are free.

A final farewell, no need to mourn,
From shadows fleeting, new dreams are born.
The journey may end, but love remains,
In the quiet release, we break our chains.

In the Hands of Time

Time trickles softly like grains of sand,
Each moment a story, a golden strand.
Within its embrace, we find our way,
As shadows lengthen, we learn to sway.

With every tick, a dance begins,
A melody woven of losses and wins.
In the pause, reflections arise,
A tapestry rich against changing skies.

Holding close the laughter and tears,
Threading the fabric of all our years.
In echoes of memories, we reside,
In the hands of time, we cannot hide.

Seasons will shift, as all things do,
Yet in our hearts, the love stays true.
With patience, we savor each fleeting spark,
As daylight breaks anew from the dark.

Time teaches softly, gently and wise,
In its hands, we learn to rise.
Embrace the journey, its twists and turns,
For in the end, it's what our heart yearns.

A Soft Letdown

When dreams dissolve in the morning light,
A gentle sigh marks the end of night.
Fleeting moments slip through my hands,
Like drifting grains in forgotten sands.

In tender whispers of a fleeting hope,
I'm learning to bend, to quietly cope.
Each promise falters, a softened dive,
Still, within me, the will to survive.

The weight of longing, a sweet refrain,
Yet hope persists amidst the pain.
A letdown softly cradles the heart,
In letting go, I find my part.

Each dusk brings lessons, each dawn a chance,
To rise anew, to change the dance.
With every heartbeat, scars will fade,
In the soft letdown, a song is made.

Life's fleeting treasures, both bittersweet,
In their embrace, I find my feet.
Though dreams may wane, resilience grows strong,
In the melody of where I belong.

Streams of Consciousness

In the river of thoughts, ideas flow,
Currents entwine where wild visions grow.
Shifting shapes like clouds in the twilight,
In streams of consciousness, we ignite.

Floating on whispers, we drift and sway,
Each moment a canvas, colors at play.
Through laughter and sorrow, we carve our paths,
With every ripple, the heart's aftermath.

Lost in the depths, where silence reigns,
I search for meaning among the pains.
The ebb and flow of a restless mind,
In these waters, solace I find.

Thoughts sparkle bright like stars on a sea,
Creating a narrative, wild and free.
Emotions cascade in a vibrant dance,
In the streams of consciousness, we take a chance.

Connected in currents, I see the light,
As dreams entwine in the calm of night.
With every thought, a world unfolds,
In the depths of our minds, our story is told.

Waves of Change

The tide rolls in with whispers soft,
Carrying dreams on its frothy crest.
Each surge unveils a tale aloft,
New paths are born, old anchors rest.

In the depths, the shadows sway,
Mirrored hopes in the ocean's dance.
Time flows on, night spills to day,
Ebbing fears, igniting chance.

Though storms may rise with furious might,
The heart is steady, anchored true.
With every wave, we gain new sight,
Navigating through paths anew.

Footprints washed by salt and brine,
Nature's rhythm guides our way.
Learning to trust in the divine,
As we ride on, come what may.

Embrace the change, let go the past,
Like sea foam frolicking in the breeze.
With every moment, hold it fast,
As we flow like waves with ease.

Painting in the Void

With a brush of silence, colors spread,
On a canvas void, dreams take flight.
Imagined worlds where thoughts are fed,
Each stroke a spark, ignites the night.

Shades of longing dance and swirl,
In the empty space, visions bloom.
As the palette whispers and twirls,
Life emerges from shadows' gloom.

Echoes of laughter, whispers of peace,
All manifest in crafted hue.
Brush-stroked memories, piece by piece,
Build a masterpiece, long overdue.

In this void, we find our voice,
Creating beauty from bare despair.
Lost in art, we learn to rejoice,
As colors blend, and fears lay bare.

The canvas breathes, the heart expands,
In the stillness, creativity flows.
Holding the future in gentle hands,
Painting in the void, life bestows.

The Last Embrace

In twilight's glow, we find our place,
As shadows dance on faded stone.
A final touch, a soft embrace,
In silence shared, we are not alone.

Memories wrapped in tender sighs,
Hold tight the moments, time slips by.
As daylight fades and evening cries,
The love we shared will never die.

Your warmth lingers like morning dew,
A lingering scent of yesterday.
Beneath the stars, the night feels new,
As echoes of laughter slowly sway.

Though distance calls, and paths may part,
In every heartbeat, you remain.
A whispered promise from the heart,
In every joy, I'll feel the pain.

With heavy hearts, we bid farewell,
Yet in this moment, we embrace.
A story etched, a tale to tell,
In love's sweet memory, time finds grace.

Breaking Chains of Memory

Crumbled whispers from days of old,
Faded echoes trapped in time.
In shadows deep, the truth unfolds,
Reclaiming life, we dare to climb.

Chains of sorrow, once tightly wound,
Now shatter softly, piece by piece.
In every heart, a warrior found,
With courage summoned, fear can cease.

From ashes rise, a phoenix bold,
As light returns, our spirits soar.
No longer shackled by what once told,
We break the chains, forevermore.

Memories shift, the past set free,
A tapestry woven with threads of gold.
In embracing change, we learn to see,
A future bright, our stories unfold.

With each step taken, a choice is made,
To heal the heart, to let love in.
From shadows cast, we will not fade,
Breaking chains, a new life to begin.

Shadows of What Once Was

Shadows linger where light once kissed,
Memories dance in the twilight mist.
Echoes of laughter in the fading light,
Haunting the silence, cloaked in night.

Cracked photo frames hold stories untold,
Fragments of life, a tapestry old.
Familiar whispers, soft as a sigh,
In the heart's chamber, they never die.

The clock ticks softly, a muted chime,
Each beat recalls a forgotten time.
In the stillness, the past comes alive,
In shadows we dwell, where memories thrive.

Beneath the stars, we search for peace,
In shadows, the echoes find their release.
With every step on this haunted ground,
The whispers of love are lost, but found.

Let the shadows leap, let them play,
For in the night, they guide our way.
What once was vibrant, now a soft glow,
In the arms of the past, we ever flow.

The Gift of Solitude

In the quiet surges, calm and wide,
Peaceful thoughts, a gentle tide.
Time slows down, like a whispered prayer,
In solitude's arms, troubles lay bare.

The heart finds peace in unspoken words,
As nature sings, the song of birds.
Moments drift by, soft as a breeze,
In stillness, a mind is put at ease.

With each breath drawn, the world fades away,
Wrapped in the warmth of a tranquil day.
The soul unravels like a silken thread,
In silence, the heart's true path is fed.

Thoughts take flight, like leaves in the air,
Creating a dance, sweet and rare.
In the realm of solitude, light is found,
In moments of stillness, we are unbound.

So cherish the gift, this precious space,
Where the mind can wander, and the spirit embrace.
In the depths of solitude, we come to know,
The beauty of self, in the gentle flow.

Unwritten Pathways

Winding roads stretch far beyond sight,
Mysteries beckon in the dimming light.
Footsteps hesitant, but spirits bold,
The journey awaits, a story unfolds.

Each choice a puzzle, each turn a chance,
Through wild ferns and nature's dance.
With the weight of dreams tucked inside,
Unwritten pathways await our stride.

In whispers of trees, we hear their call,
Nature speaks softly, inviting us all.
Beneath the stars, the night is bright,
Unseen barriers vanish from sight.

With every sigh and every breath,
Life sketches paths, a dance with death.
Step by step, we forge our way,
In the tapestry of night and day.

What lies ahead, no map can show,
In the heart's compass, the truth will grow.
Adventure awaits past the horizon's glow,
On unwritten pathways, together we go.

Blossoms in the Breeze

Delicate petals in the spring's sweet air,
Dance with the wind, without a care.
Colors collide in a vibrant display,
Nature's canvas, come out to play.

Beneath the sun's warm, golden touch,
Every blossom unveils so much.
Nature's laughter, a gentle tease,
In the garden's heart, the soul finds ease.

A soft fragrance weaves through the day,
Guiding our senses as we sway.
Each bloom a story, each leaf a song,
In the warmth of spring, where we belong.

With every breeze, new treasures arise,
Whispers of hope in the infinite skies.
In the realm of blooms, we breathe in deep,
Among the petals, our dreams we keep.

As seasons shift and colors wane,
In memories of blossoms, we exist again.
For in the breeze, love's essence sways,
In gardens of life, we spend our days.

Milton Keynes UK
Ingram Content Group UK Ltd.
UKHW021522011224
451733UK00007B/120